How We Use

Rubber

Chris Oxlade

www.raintreepublishers.co.uk
Visit our website to find out more information about **Raintree** books.

To order:
☎ Phone 44 (0) 1865 888112
▤ Send a fax to 44 (0) 1865 314091
▣ Visit the Raintree bookshop at **www.raintreepublishers.co.uk** to browse our catalogue and order online.

First published in Great Britain by Raintree,
Halley Court, Jordan Hill, Oxford OX2 8EJ,
part of Harcourt Education.
Raintree is a registered trademark of Harcourt
Education Ltd.

Editorial: Nicholas Hunter and Richard Woodham
Design: Kim Saar and Bridge Creative Services Ltd
Picture Research: Maria Joannou and Debra Weatherley
Production: Amanda Meaden
Indexing: Indexing Specialists (UK) Ltd

Originated by Ambassador Litho Ltd
Printed and bound in Hong Kong, China by
South China Printing Company

ISBN 1 844 43438 9
09 08 07 06 05
10 9 8 7 6 5 4 3 2 1

British Library Cataloguing in Publication Data
Oxlade, Chris
How We Use Rubber. – (Using Materials)
620.1'94
A full catalogue record for this book is available from
the British Library.

Acknowledgements
The publishers would like to thank the following for
permission to reproduce photographs: Alamy Images
pp. **14**, **27**; Alvey & Towers p. **15**; Art Directors & Trip
pp. **6**, **7** (J. Wakelin), **26** (D. Hastilow), **29** (B. Turner);
Corbis pp. **5** (Harcourt Index), **20** (Volker Möhrke),
23 (Harcourt Index); Gareth Boden p. **25**; Oxford
Scientific Films p. **22** (Daybreak Imagery); Photodisc
pp. **8** (Harcourt Index), **i**, **21** (Harcourt Index);
photographersdirect.com pp. **9** (The Picture Source),
19 (Alan Spence), **24** (JRCpix.com/Jonah Calinawan);
Powerstock pp. **12** (Pixel), **16** (Pixel); Robert Harding
Picture Library p. **10**; Science Photo Library pp. **4** (Tony
Craddock), **11** (Maximillian Stock Ltd), **13** (Professor
Harold Edgerton), **17** (Martyn F. Chillmaid), **18**
(Novosti Press Agency); Sutton Motorsport p. **28**.

Cover photograph of tread on a rubber tyre,
reproduced with permission of Rex Features.

Every effort has been made to contact copyright
holders of any material reproduced in this book. Any
omissions will be rectified in subsequent printings if
notice is given to the publishers.

The paper used to print this book comes from
sustainable resources.

Contents

Any words appearing in bold, **like this**, are explained in the Glossary.

Rubber and its properties

All the things we use are made from materials. Rubber is a material. We use rubber for many different jobs. Tyres for cars and buses are made from rubber. **Elastic** bands, tennis balls, rubber gloves, toys for pets, **washers**, plugs and cushions are all made from rubber, too.

Rubber is used to make balloons.

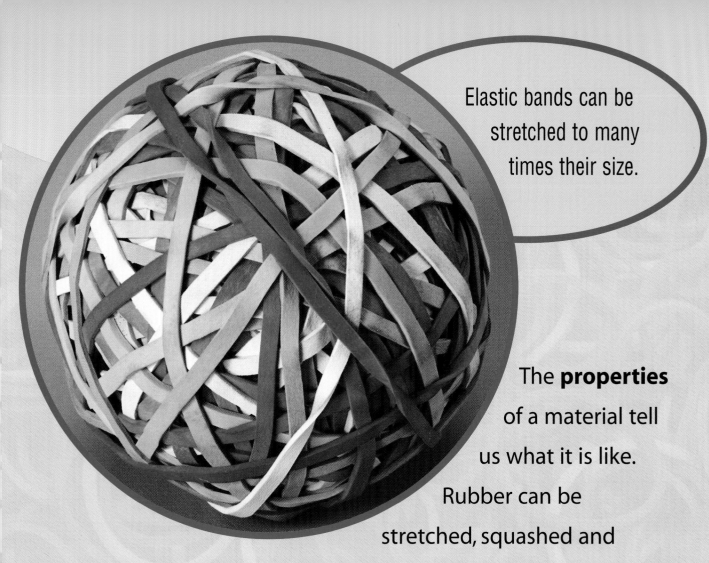

Elastic bands can be stretched to many times their size.

The **properties** of a material tell us what it is like. Rubber can be stretched, squashed and bent. It is also tough and hard-wearing. Rubber is **waterproof** and **airtight**. It is also an **insulator**, which means it does not let electricity flow through it.

Don't use it!

The different properties of materials make them useful for some jobs. The properties also make them unsuitable for other jobs. For example, rubber is bendy, so we don't make knives from rubber. They would not cut anything!

Where does rubber come from?

Some of the rubber we use is natural. It comes from trees called rubber trees that grow in **tropical** areas of the world. Rubber is part of a **liquid** called **latex** found in the bark of these trees. Latex is a mixture of rubber and water. Thousands of rubber trees are grown in **plantations** to produce latex.

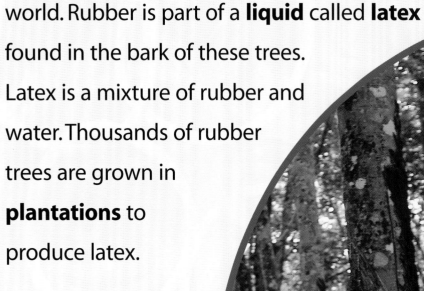

This picture shows how latex is collected from rubber trees growing in a plantation.

Natural rubber must be rolled to squeeze out the water.

Collecting latex from a tree is called tapping. Workers cut grooves in the bark of rubber trees. The latex seeps out of the bark and slowly runs down the grooves into cups. **Chemicals** are added to the latex which make the rubber gather together in lumps. The liquid is **strained** to remove the lumps of rubber. The rubber is then pressed and dried to make sheets which are ready to be made into rubber objects.

Rubber in the past

*People have known about rubber for hundreds of years. One of its first uses was for rubbing out pencil marks. This is where the word rubber comes from. Rubber became even more useful when scientists worked out how to make it tougher. It could then be used to make tough **waterproof** seals inside machines.*

Synthetic rubber

Natural rubber is an important material, but most rubber we use today is not natural. It is made in factories from **chemicals**. It is called **synthetic** rubber. The chemicals used to make synthetic rubber come from **crude oil**, which is found under the ground and under the sea bed.

This rig brings crude oil from under the sea bed to the surface.

These lumps of synthetic rubber will be used to make many different rubber items.

Rubber factories use different mixtures of chemicals to make different sorts of rubber. Most synthetic rubber is called general-purpose rubber. Scientists are always trying to make synthetic rubbers with new and better **properties**. These are called special rubbers. A special rubber might be designed to withstand very high temperatures in an oven or very low temperatures in a freezer.

Don't use it!
*General-purpose synthetic rubber and natural rubber are harmed by some substances. **Gases**, oils and sunlight make them weaken and crack. We must use special rubbers for jobs where it will touch these substances, such as in a gas pipe.*

Working with rubber

Rubber comes from the factory in lumps or sheets. Before rubber is made into objects, it is turned into a soft lump by heating and stirring it. Other substances can be added to the rubber to change its **properties**. These can make it more **elastic** or tougher. The soft rubber is then turned into objects.

Rubber gloves like these are made by dipping hand-shaped moulds into liquid rubber.

This sheet of rubber is ready to be cut into shapes.

Objects such as tyres and hot-water bottles are made by pressing soft rubber into a **mould**. The hole in the mould is the same shape as the object. Tubes and door seals are made by pushing soft rubber through a hole. This is called extruding. **Washers** and mats are made by cutting shapes from rubber sheets.

Making rubber tough

*To make rubber harder and tougher, it is heated with a **chemical** called sulphur and then cooled again. This process is called **vulcanization**. Almost all the rubber we use is vulcanized.*

Elastic rubber

Rubber is an **elastic** material. This means you can stretch, squash or bend it. Rubber will also go back to its original shape when you let go. You can stretch, squash or bend a piece of rubber thousands of times without it breaking. This **property** makes rubber suitable for thousands of jobs.

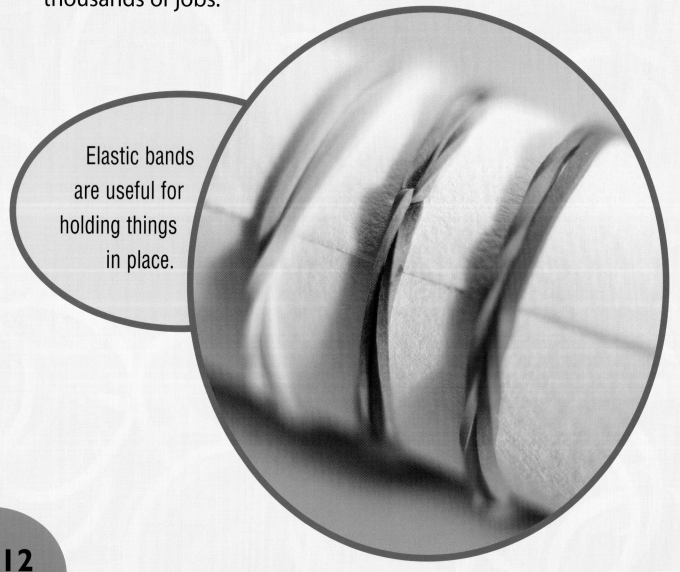

Elastic bands are useful for holding things in place.

A rubber ball is squashed as it hits the ground.

A rubber band can stretch to many times its original length without breaking. The rubber used in a tennis ball is squashed as it hits the ground. It can then spring back into its original shape, making it bounce. Rubber is also used to make elastic cord for clothes and elastic bandages.

Don't use it!

Being elastic is a very useful property of rubber. For many jobs, however, we want a material that does not stretch, so we cannot use rubber. For example, we don't use rubber to make road bridges.

13

Shock-absorbing rubber

If you hit a piece of rubber with a hammer, the hammer bounces off without damaging it. We say that rubber is **shock-absorbent**. For example, running shoes have soles made of a **synthetic** rubber that has been designed to absorb shocks as your feet hit the ground.

We protect objects from shocks with rubber. Some mobile telephones and torches are covered in a layer of rubber. The telephone or torch will be protected by the·rubber if it is dropped.

Shoes worn by basketball players absorb shocks all the time during a game.

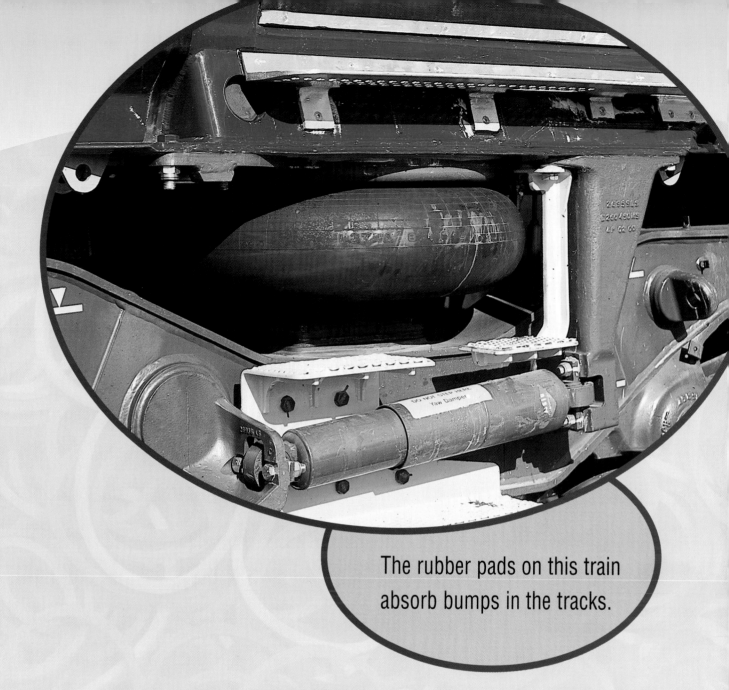

The rubber pads on this train absorb bumps in the tracks.

Some cars have special rubber parts that absorb shocks as the vehicle goes over bumps in the road. This gives the passengers a comfortable ride. Vehicles have hundreds of other rubber parts. For example, the engine sits on special rubber pads. These stop vibrations from the engine reaching the passengers.

Rubber for grip

When two surfaces touch or move against each other, a force called **friction** tries to stop the surfaces sliding past each other. Different materials cause different amounts of friction. Rubber's softness is one **property** that makes it cause lots of friction when it touches or moves against another material.

Tools such as hammers and drills often have rubber grips. The friction between your hand and the grip makes it easy to hold the tool firmly. Non-slip floor mats have rubber backing. The rubber grips the floor, stopping a mat from sliding when you step on it.

The rubber grip on this hammer creates friction.

Rubber pads are used to slow most vehicles, from bicycles to racing cars.

Rubber stops your bicycle when you pull on the brakes. The blocks of rubber press against the metal rims of the wheels. The friction slows the wheels until you stop.

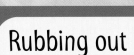

Rubbing out

A pencil eraser is made of rubber. Rubbing the paper with the eraser wears away the surface of the paper that the pencil marks are on. This leaves fresh blank paper to write on.

Rubber tyres

Nearly half of all the rubber produced is made into tyres for cars, trucks, bicycles and other vehicles. Because rubber is **elastic**, rubber tyres help smooth out the bumps in the road. Rubber tyres also grip the road, stopping a vehicle from sliding as it goes round corners. Rubber is hard-wearing so tyres last a long time even though they roll along rough roads.

The huge tyres on this truck smooth out rough roads.

The inner tube can be seen in this cross-section of a bicycle tyre.

A car tyre is made of rubber, strong **fabric** and steel wire. The fabric and wire stop the tyre from bursting if it gets a puncture. Bicycle tyres have rubber inner tubes inside. When you pump up a bicycle's tyres, air goes into the inner tube. Some tyres on trucks and buses have rubber inner tubes too.

Don't use it!

Because rubber is good at gripping, we don't use it to make things that we want to be slippery. So we would not use rubber to make a playground slide.

Tough rubber

Rubber is a good material for vehicle tyres because it is tough. It also lasts a long time. We say that rubber is hard-wearing. This **property** of rubber makes it useful for making many objects.

Wipers for car windscreens are made from strips of rubber held along one edge by metal or plastic. The rubber strip wipes water off the glass, drying it. Rubber is bendy and soft, so the wiper can press hard on the glass without scratching it.

Because rubber is hard-wearing, wiper blades last a long time.

Rubber boats can hit rocks and not be damaged. A wooden boat would be wrecked on rocks like these.

Toys for dogs are made from rubber. Because the rubber is soft, the dog can hold the toy without damaging its teeth. Because the rubber is hard-wearing, the toy lasts a long time even if the dog chews it.

Waterproof rubber

Rubber is **waterproof** and **airtight**. This means that water and air cannot pass through it. Rubber can be used to keep **liquids** and **gases** in and out of places.

Keeping things out

People wear rubber gloves to stop harmful **chemicals** in cleaning materials from touching their skin. Rubber boots keep your feet dry when it is wet. A layer of rubber can be put on clothes to make them waterproof.

This fisherman is wearing waders made from a waterproof fabric.

A bendy rubber hose carries water from a tap out into a garden.

Keeping things in

A rubber hot-water bottle keeps you warm on a cold night. The tough, thick rubber means that the bottle does not burst or leak. Rubber tubes are easy to bend around corners. We use them to carry water in washing machines and engines. Hoses on fire engines are made from a strong **fabric** which is coated with rubber.

Sealing with rubber

Rubber is **waterproof**, **airtight**, bendy and tough. These **properties** mean rubber is a good material for making stoppers and seals. These are pieces of rubber that hold **liquids** and **gases** in one place.

Rubber stoppers are used to stop liquid spilling from bottles. The rubber squashes slightly to give a tight fit. Airtight rubber seals on the lids of jars keep food fresh. Sink and bath plugs are made from rubber, too.

This rubber seal fits tightly against the glass tube.

The rubber used in ovens must be able to withstand high temperatures.

An oven has a rubber strip between the door and the cabinet that stops hot air escaping. A fridge has a seal that stops warm air getting in. Car doors have rubber seals that stop water getting in between the door and the car body. Rubber seals around doors in houses stop draughts.

Rubber and electricity

*Rubber is a good electrical **insulator**. That means it does not let electricity flow through it. Rubber is sometimes used to insulate wires and cables. This means we can touch them safely without getting an electric shock.*

Sponge and foam rubber

Sponge rubber and foam rubber contain millions of tiny bubbles. Because they are mostly made of bubbles, they are very soft, springy and light.

Sponge rubber is made by adding special **chemicals** to the rubber. When the rubber is put into a **mould** and heated, the chemicals make **gases** that form bubbles. We use sponge rubber to make wetsuits. The bubbles in the rubber trap warm air around a person's body.

Wetsuits keep surfers warm in the cold water.

Foam rubber is used inside these cushions to make them soft and comfortable.

Don't use it!

Sponge rubber and foam rubber are very squashy and not very hard-wearing. So we don't use them to make rubber objects that need to be tough, such as tyres.

Foam rubber is made by whipping **liquid** rubber. This mixes air into the rubber, making it frothy. The mixture is put into moulds where it sets, trapping the air. It is **vulcanized** to make it tougher. We use foam rubber to make cushions, mattresses, pillows and soft packaging.

Rubber and the environment

Rubber does not rot like wood or paper. If we throw rubber away it will stay in the ground for thousands of years. Making **synthetic** rubber also uses up precious **chemicals** from **crude oil**.

Re-using rubber

We can **re-use** old rubber tyres. Worn truck tyres are given a new layer of rubber so they can be used again. Whole tyres are made into crash barriers, playground swings and garden containers. Tyres are cut up to make rubber shapes. These are made into soles for shoes, supports for young trees and water containers.

Rubber tyres helped save the driver of this car from injury.

The surface of this playground is made from recycled rubber tyres.

Recycling rubber

Old tyres are also **recycled** into new rubber products. Old rubber is hard to turn into fresh rubber. Instead, tyres are broken into small lumps to make a material called crumb rubber. This is added to fresh rubber to make many different rubber objects, such as mats, tiles and non-slip surfaces for playgrounds and running tracks.

Find out for yourself

The best way to find out more about rubber is to investigate it for yourself. Look around your home for things made from rubber, and keep an eye out for rubber during your day. Think about why rubber was used for each job. What properties make it suitable? You will find the answers to many of your questions in this book. You can also look in other books and on the Internet.

Books to read

Science Answers: Grouping Materials, Carol Ballard (Heinemann Library, 2003)

Discovering Science: Matter, Rebecca Hunter (Raintree, 2003)

Materials and their Properties, Angela Royston (Heinemann Library, 2003)

Using the Internet

Try searching the Internet to find out about things to do with rubber. Websites can change, so if some of the links below no longer work, don't worry. Use a search engine, such as www.yahooligans.com or www.internet4kids.com. You could try searching using the keywords 'rubber plantation', 'rubber tyres' and 'crumb rubber'. Here are some websites to get you started.

Websites

A great site, which explains all about different materials: http://www.bbc.co.uk/schools/revisewise/science/materials/

Find out more about the properties of different materials: http://www.strangematterexhibit.com

Glossary

airtight type of material that does not let air pass through it

chemical substance that we use to make other substances, or for jobs such as cleaning

crude oil oil as it is found naturally in the ground

elastic able to stretch and return to its original shape

fabric flat, bendy piece of material, made from woven fibres

friction force that tries to stop two surfaces sliding past each other

gas something in a state where it spreads out to fill all the space it can

insulator type of material that does not let electricity flow through it

latex liquid from a rubber tree that natural rubber is made from

liquid something in a runny state that can be poured from one container to another

mould hollow shape that hot, soft rubber is pressed into to make an object

plantation area of land where trees are farmed by people

property characteristic or quality of a material

recycle use again

re-use use an object again after it has been used once

shock-absorbent able to take in and smooth out sudden shocks and bumps

strain pour through a sieve to separate a solid from a liquid

synthetic material that is not natural

tropical from the tropics, which is an area of the world near the equator

vulcanization making rubber tougher by heating it with sulphur

washer flat, round piece of rubber that stops water leaking from a tap

waterproof material that does not let water pass through it

Index

Titles in the *Using Materials* series include:

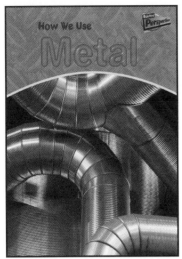

Hardback   1 844 43436 2

Hardback   1 844 43437 0

Hardback   1 844 43438 9

Hardback   1 844 43439 7

Hardback   1 844 43440 0

Hardback   1 844 43441 9

Find out about the other titles in this series on our website www.raintreepublishers.co.uk